THE PARABLES
OF
OUR LORD AND SAVIOUR
JESUS CHRIST

THE PARABLES

OF

OUR LORD AND SAVIOUR
JESUS CHRIST

with pictures by
JOHN EVERETT MILLAIS

engraved by
THE BROTHERS DALZIEL

with a new introduction by
MARY LUTYENS

DOVER PUBLICATIONS, INC., NEW YORK

This Dover edition, first published in 1975, is an unabridged republication of the work originally engraved by the Brothers Dalziel and published by Routledge, Warne, and Routledge, in London in 1864. Mary Lutyens has written a new Introduction especially for the Dover edition.

International Standard Book Number: 0-486-20494-4
Library of Congress Catalog Card Number: 74-20328

Manufactured in the United States of America
Dover Publications, Inc.
180 Varick Street
New York, N.Y. 10014

CONTENTS.

INTRODUCTION TO
THE DOVER EDITION

JOHN EVERETT MILLAIS, BORN
JUNE 8, 1829; DIED AUGUST 13, 1896;
CREATED A BARONET 1885; ELECTED
PRESIDENT OF THE ROYAL ACA-
DEMY JANUARY, 1896.

Millais was twenty-eight when in the autumn of 1857 he accepted a commission from the engravers, the Dalziel brothers, to illustrate a book of the Parables of Our Lord. Millais undertook to produce thirty drawings, and the Dalziels hoped to publish the book the following summer. Millais took so long, however, to make his designs that the Dalziels were obliged to release him from ten of them; even so, the book did not appear until the end of 1863.

In July 1855 Millais had married Effie Gray, who, the year before, had obtained an annulment from John Ruskin after six years of unconsummated marriage and had resumed her maiden name. The first of Millais's eight children, a boy, had been born in 1856 and his second son was born just a month after his accepting the Dalziels' commission. Effie had no money of her own, her father, George Gray, a solicitor in Perth, having brought himself to the verge of bankruptcy by railway speculation, nor was Ruskin giving her any alimony. Millais's parents, living in a cottage near London, were of modest means, so on Millais fell the whole burden of supporting his wife and his increasing family by his art.

An infant prodigy, trained at the Royal Academy Schools for ten years from the age of eleven, Millais had carried off every Academy medal. In 1848, with Holman Hunt, Dante Gabriel Rossetti and four others, he had founded the Pre-Raphaelite Brotherhood, a close-knit group of friends of

more or less the same age whose object was to bring nature back to art—
to paint what they saw, to move right away from the conventional studio
picture of the day. Although they continued to paint their human figures
in the studio, their backgrounds, birds, animals, flowers and trees were all
painted out of doors, irrespective of the weather. Their pictures were anything but impressionistic. Every leaf, feather, petal and blade of grass was
painted from life with meticulous fidelity, in the belief that such perfection of detail must give a sense of reality. Moreover, in reaction against
the coating of brown varnish that was then the conventional attribute of
all exhibits at the Royal Academy, they painted in bright jewel colours
on a canvas first prepared with a white ground, so that even today their
pictures startle by their brilliance. These early Pre-Raphaelite canvases,
though so lovable to those who are touched by them, are entirely lacking
in the appearance of nature for which the Brothers strove.

It is surprising that such revolutionary productions were ever accepted
by the Royal Academy for exhibition, and not at all surprising that they
were damned by the critics. In 1851, so fierce were the attacks that
Holman Hunt was on the point of giving up art and emigrating to the
gold fields of Australia when Ruskin, even then the most influential critic
of his day, came to their rescue with two letters to *The Times*. Ruskin
had never met any of the Brothers, but detailed painting from nature was
his *credo*, and the second volume of his *Modern Painters*, published in
1846, had been the Brotherhood's original inspiration. The *Times* letters
led to a meeting, and Millais in particular became Ruskin's protégé. From
that time onwards it seemed that Millais's success was assured, especially
when in 1853, at the earliest possible age, he was elected an Associate
Member of the Royal Academy. By this time the original Pre-Raphaelite
Brotherhood had broken up though its influence was so widespread that
many followers and younger artists, such as Burne-Jones, are still referred
to as Pre-Raphaelites.

When Millais fell in love with Ruskin's wife while the three of them
were on holiday together in the Highlands in 1853, and then married her
two years later, Millais was faced with the probability of losing Ruskin's
patronage, a circumstance which might well have ruined his now promis-
ing career. Ruskin was not the man, however, to allow his artistic judge-
ment to be influenced by personal feelings and in his *Academy Notes* for
1855 and 1856 he praised Millais exaggeratedly: "Titian himself could
hardly head him now," he wrote in 1856. When, therefore, Millais's main
picture for 1857, "Sir Isumbras at the Ford," was condemned by Ruskin
as well as by other important critics, Millais was all the more mortified

since he could not attribute Ruskin's opinion to anything personal. Because of the critics' abuse (". . . the change in his manner . . . is not merely Fall, it is Catastrophe," Ruskin pronounced in his *Academy Notes*) Millais had great difficulty in selling his pictures that year and was, therefore, all the more ready to accept any work offered to him. The next three years were probably the most unhappy and insecure of his professional life, until with the triumph of "The Black Brunswicker" in 1860 his confidence was fully restored. His success with the public then became so great that he could disregard all critical opprobrium.

Already in the first year of his marriage Millais had accepted commissions for book illustrations, an art at which he came to excel. He was responsible for eighteen of the fifty-four wood-engravings for Moxon's illustrated edition of Tennyson's poems which appeared in 1857, and of these eighteen, eight had been engraved by the Dalziels.

There were three brothers and a sister in this well-known firm of wood-engravers—George, Edward, John and Margaret— though which of the three brothers it was that Millais addressed as "My dear Dalziel" in his letters is uncertain. The Dalziel brothers had set up in business in London in 1839, and thereafter, until 1893 when the firm broke up, they engraved the work of most of the famous artists of the day.

In wood-engraving, a process introduced into England by Thomas Bewick (1753–1827), the design is drawn onto a section of boxwood cut against the grain. The engraver's task is to gouge out with a burin or graver (a sharp, oblique-edged tool used for engraving on metal) all the wood that is not to appear in print, leaving the lines of the drawing in relief. Thus it is the reverse of the intaglio process of engraving on metal. The wood-engraver can cut such fine lines in the surface of the block that in cross-hatching they have the appearance of an etching.

Boxwood is so extremely hard that it can stand great pressure; it was, therefore, found to be more suitable for large editions than the delicate copper plates. It was also much cheaper, so that by the 1860's books and periodicals with good illustrations became available to the public for the first time, and their quality created a demand that was met by the publication of a number of new magazines.

It is the use of the burin and the end grain of hard wood that distinguishes wood-engraving from woodcutting. For a woodcut a lengthways plane of soft wood sliced along the grain is used and cut with a knife. But for both woodcutting and wood-engraving it is the part left in relief that is inked for printing. As box is a small tree, only small blocks can be made from it; for large illustrations two or several blocks had to be screwed together. This method had the advantage, though, of saving time when a deadline had to be met, for the blocks could be unscrewed and given out to several engravers and then screwed together again. The Parable engravings were each drawn on a single block of boxwood the size of the illustrations in this volume (about the largest that can be made from box), ⅞ inch thick.

When the artist was also the engraver, as in the case of Thomas Bewick, he could adapt his drawings to the limitations of the medium. To engrave the work of artists, however, who had little idea of the difficulties of such a delicate process was another art altogether, one which reached its peak with the Dalziels and a few other engravers of the period before photography came into general use for book illustrations. Millais was deeply appreciative of the Dalziels' work and always endeavoured to adapt his designs to it, unlike Rossetti who was constantly enraged with them for spoiling fuzzy drawings of his which it was virtually impossible for any engraver to cut satisfactorily. The Dalziels' signature, which can be seen at the bottom of all their engravings, was expressively referred to by Rossetti as "Dalziel's cannibal jig."

When the Dalziels chose Millais to illustrate the Parables, they considered that not only was he an artist of high quality but that he could be relied upon to treat the subject with sufficient dignity yet avoid the old conventional style of Biblical art. In the first edition of the book, it is stated that Millais made his first drawing in August 1857. This is not quite accurate; it was then that he accepted the commission, writing on 13 August: "I shall be very glad to accept your offer, but you must give me time. One great inducement for me to undertake these illustrations is the fact that the book will be entirely illustrated by me alone, the subject is quite to my liking; you could not have chosen anything more congenial to my desire. I would set about them immediately if you would send me some wood blocks. Will you send me a list of the Parables or leave it to me? I would prefer the former [a list was sent to him]. There is so much labour in these drawings that I trust you will give me my own time, otherwise I could not undertake the commission; I shall make it a labour of love like yourselves."

Millais received 20 pounds each for these drawings. As he had received 15 pounds each for the much smaller Tennyson drawings (none of the Tennysons measured as much as four inches), this work was poorly paid though not exactly "a labour of love." It had one great advantage, though, to Millais: whereas all the Tennyson drawings had been destroyed in the cutting, he made water-colour drawings of most of his

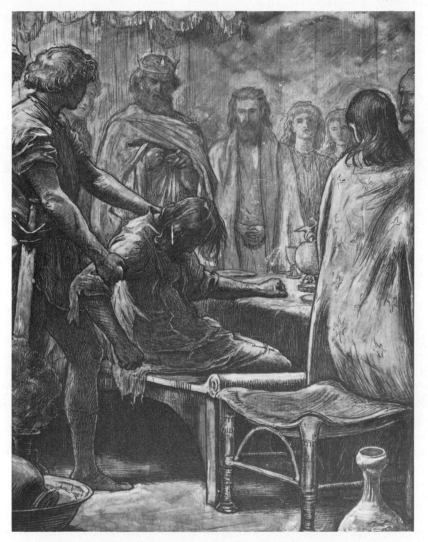

Fig. 1. "The Marriage Feast": original drawing on wood block in pen and ink on background of Chinese white, 5½ × 4¼ in. (Victoria and Albert Museum)

designs for the Parables which he was able to sell separately. Indeed, two of them, "The Lost Piece of Silver" and "The Tares," he worked up into oil paintings. The former, which was exhibited at the Royal Academy in 1862, had an unfortunate history. Millais gave it to the sculptor Baron Carlo Marochetti in exchange for a marble bust of Effie by this once famous Italian artist who worked in London. One day there was a gas explosion in the Baron's house in Onslow Square, and the picture, frame and all, was shot through the window and completely destroyed. Fortunately there is a water-colour version of it in the Fogg Art Museum, Cambridge. It is remarkable how in the engraving (page 55) Dalziel has managed to show the girl's skin, illuminated by the candle, shining through the flimsy material of her sleeve. She bears such a distinct resemblance to Effie that one may conclude Effie was the model.

Proofs on India paper of four of the engravings, under the Dalziels' name, were exhibited at the Royal Academy in 1862, and another four the following year. Several proofs were also on show at the 1862 International Exhibition at South Kensington. Twelve of the illustrations were published in monthly parts in the magazine *Good Words* throughout 1863, illustrating a series of articles, "The Parables in the Light of the Present Day" by the Reverend Thomas Guthrie. The Dalziels, who owned the copyright of the engravings, sold them to *Good Words* for 1,000 pounds, but in order to preserve the wood blocks for the book, they were printed in electrotype, a more recent and complicated invention than stereotype, though for both processes a wax mould had to be made from the engraved block and then cast in metal. The impressions from these casts were not as clear as those printed direct from the wood. In 1876, fourteen of the designs were used for a stained-glass window presented by Effie's father to the parish church of Kinnoull, Perth, in memory of Effie's and Millais's second son who died that year from typhoid at the age of nineteen. The window gives a glow to this otherwise stark kirk on the banks of the Tay.

For the engravings Millais drew his designs in reverse straight onto the wood block. He drew in ink or lamp black, or sometimes pencil, onto a surface prepared with Chinese white. Four of his original drawings on the wood are still in existence—"The Marriage Feast" (Victoria and Albert Museum), "The Unmerciful Servant" (Museum of Fine Arts, Boston), "The Importunate Friend" and "The Good Shepherd" (both at the Johannesburg Art Gallery). Millais did not make his drawings in the order in which they appear in the book except for "The Good Shepherd" which, the last in the book, happened to be the last to be engraved. It was

Fig. 2. "The Unmerciful Servant": photograph of original drawing on wood block before it was cut (Collection of R. V. Craig)

not cut until October or November 1863, and "The Marriage Feast" not until shortly before that date; it seems likely, therefore, that the other two drawings which have survived on the wood must also have been among the last to be cut, for their survival shows that already by 1863 the Dalziels were using photography to transfer a drawing from one block to another for cutting. This enabled them to sell the first blocks as original Millais drawings. "The Marriage Feast" (Fig. 1) was acquired by the Victoria and Albert Museum direct from the Dalziels for 20 pounds in 1884; "The Unmerciful Servant" (formerly in the Hartley Collection) was probably acquired by Harold Hartley from Gilbert, John Dalziel's son, and the blocks in Johannesburg have Dalziel's name written on the back. It may be noticed in Fig. 1 how the grain of the wood is showing through the white ground after more than a hundred years.

In the history of the Dalziels' firm it is stated, "After spending much time and labour in experimenting, as well as spoiling a great many blocks, we succeeded in getting fairly good photographs for the engraver's purpose on other pieces of wood, and so the valuable original drawings were preserved." No definite date is given for the attainment of this success, but one may well believe that the four illustrations mentioned above were the first ever to be produced in England by the new invention.

Photographs of three of the original drawings on wood taken by the Dalziels before the blocks were engraved and inscribed to that effect by Gilbert Dalziel have recently come to light—"The Wicked Husbandmen," "The Unjust Judge" and "The Unmerciful Servant" (Fig. 2). In comparing Figs. 1 and 2 with the engravings, pages 48 and 20, it can be appreciated how carefully Millais drew in reverse. The men's swords in both reverse drawings hang on the right so that they will appear correctly on the left in the engravings. In Fig. 1, the King is pointing with his left index finger and the man next to him has his left thumb clasped over his right so that it will appear right over left in the illustration in the way the majority of men clasp their hands. In Fig. 2, the centre figure is holding his sword in his left hand and the master is cogitating with his left hand up to his mouth. Millais made no mistakes in reverse drawing in any of the Parables, and that at a time when many artists undertaking book and magazine illustrations did not bother about such details. So long as their signatures were the right way round, men's coats could be crossed over from right to left like a woman's, wedding rings worn on the wrong hand and scribes made to appear left-handed.

Something else may be noticed about "The Marriage Feast" drawing. It does not illustrate Luke's Parable of the Marriage Feast but that of the

Fig. 3.   "The Pearl of Great Price": drawing in pen and ink and water-colour, 6¼ × 4¾ in. (British Museum)

Marriage of the King's Son (Matthew's version of the Parable, XXII, ii-xiv): the host is a king and the servant is in the act of seizing the guest without "a wedding garment." It is evident that Millais was under the impression that this was the Parable he was illustrating. When the book was published one reviewer commented on the error and, whether because of that or because they noticed it themselves, the Dalziels at some time removed the text of the Parable of the Marriage Feast from the book and substituted that of the Marriage of the King's Son, without altering the list of contents, the caption to the illustration or the date of publication. It was easy to do this as the book was not stitched but merely stuck with gutta-percha. The Dover edition reproduces this corrected printing, so that the version of the Parable facing the illustration is the correct one.

In the edition of 1882, brought out by the Society for the Promotion of Christian Knowledge, both Parables were included. If any reader happens to pick up a second-hand copy of the 1864 edition he will be able to tell from this Parable whether or not the volume was one of the first to be issued.

Although Effie brought no dowry to Millais, her father's house provided him with a happy home in Scotland when he was not working in London—Bowerswell (pronounced Bower's Well) at Perth on the east side of the River Tay, a little way up the hill of Kinnoull. This solid stone house, dating from 1847, is still standing. There the fishing and shooting which Millais so loved were easily procurable. Effie was the eldest of eight surviving children, and her two younger sisters, Sophie and Alice, were frequently used as models by Millais as was Effie herself. Alice can been seen as the girl in "The Pearl of Great Price" (Fig. 3).

Most of the Parable drawings were executed in Scotland, and, according to Millais's youngest son who wrote his biography, the backgrounds were, in the 1890's, still recognisable views of the country round Bowerswell. A few of the backgrounds seem recognisable even today.

The reason Millais was so long in turning out the Parable designs was that he was working on many other things at the same time. Of first importance, of course, were his paintings for the Academy, and then he had accepted many other commissions for book and magazine illustrations, all of which were engraved either by the Dalziels or by their chief rival, Joseph Swain. There was Anthony Trollope's *Framley Parsonage*, with six illustrations by Millais which appeared in the *Cornhill Magazine*, followed by the same author's *The Small House at Allington* with

Fig. 4.   Photograph of 1858 or 1859 showing actual wall of Balhousie Castle used as background for "The Love of James I of Scotland." Model's hand shows through window. Compare with "The Wicked Husbandmen."

sixteen illustrations, then *Orley Farm* with thirty-three, as well as contributions to two books produced by the Dalziels, and many illustrations for serials, poems and short stories in *Good Words*, *Once a Week*, the *Cornhill*, *London Society* and the *Illustrated London News*. The Parable drawings became more and more of a burden to Millais, as his letters written to the Dalziels in the course of the work clearly show.

These letters were published by the Dalziels in facsimile in 1902 together with the twenty Parable illustrations. Although it is stated in this volume that the letters were arranged so that each should precede the picture to which it related, this was not invariably done; moreover, as the illustrations were placed in the same order as in the 1864 edition, it is not easy to work out the chronology of their execution, especially as several letters are undated and some references in dated letters are to unidentified Parables. However, an attempt has been made here to give the order in which Millais sent in the blocks to the Dalziels:

"The Good Samaritan"
"The Prodigal Son"
"The Pharisee and Publican"
"The Unjust Judge"
"The Foolish Virgins"
"The Leaven"
"The Hidden Treasure"
"The Lost Piece of Silver" (?)
"The Tares" (?)
"The Pearl of Great Price"
"The Sower"
"The Wise and Foolish Virgins"
"The Labourers in the Vineyard"
"The Rich Man and Lazarus"
"The Lost Sheep"
"The Wicked Husbandmen"
"The Unmerciful Servant" (?)
"The Importunate Friend" (?)
"The Marriage Feast"
"The Good Shepherd"

Millais was writing to Dalziel from Bowerswell on 21 October 1857, two months after accepting the commission: "Just a line to tell you I am about the Parables. Two I have got half way through & only wait models, which I shall get next week in London—I find the extra size takes up much more time as I drawings [*sic*] careful backgrounds to the illustrations. The three I have commenced with are The Good Samaritan, The Prodigal Son & Pharisee & Publican. Some of the subjects should certainly have two illustrations in place of Parables that do not admit of illustration." In the event it was only the Parable of the Virgins for which he made two illustrations.

At that time Millais had a London studio in Langham Chambers, near Portland Place, which he shared with a friend, but by the end of the year he had taken a furnished house, 16 York Terrace, Regent's Park, from where he wrote to Dalziel on 13 January 1858 about the first proofs: "I am *delighted* with the cutting of the three Parables, there are however a few corrections to each which will materially improve them—Such parts as the finger nails want rendering with greater delicasy—I will call next *Saturday* evening, & we will look over together the alterations." The fingernails evidently refer to "The Prodigal Son" (page 57). The fingernails of both father and son are clearly delineated in this engraving as are also the father's toenails. It is quite a puzzle, though, to distinguish which head is which.

By September of that year Millais had evidently finished the drawing of "The Unjust Judge" and was writing from Bowerswell on 5 October to apologise for his tardiness: "I am ashamed of myself but really I have felt it impossible to set to work on the blocks until now, and I will get on as fast as I can with them . . . nothing hinders me from the work—the evenings too are getting shorter & I have consequently less time to paint, & more time to draw—I have been painting out of doors a great deal & have been quite exhausted after the exertion, & unfit for any other work. I have many designs ready for the Parables so I can set to work on more than one—By the way I should like to have proof of the Judge block if cut."

The outdoor pictures which had so exhausted Millais were those he was working on for the 1859 Royal Academy Exhibition—"The Vale of Rest," two nuns digging a grave in the garden at Bowerswell, "Apple Blossom" and "The Love of James I of Scotland," with a background of Balhousie Castle, Perth. He had exhibited nothing at the Academy in 1858, so these pictures for 1859 were especially important to him.

He was delighted with the cutting of "The Unjust Judge" (page 67). "Nothing can be more exquisitely rendered than the 'Importunate Widow' [as he called it]," he wrote from Bowerswell on 14 January 1859. "There are two or three little trifles wh. I will tell you when I come up [one always goes *up* to London]. It appears to me even better cut than any of the others I have ever seen. . . . The two I am about are the 'Ten Virgins'—I will try & send you one next week—I am only sorry that I cannot turn them out faster—I am charmed with your work."

He did "The Foolish Virgins" first but seems to have done six others before finishing "The Wise and Foolish Virgins." Even "The Foolish Virgins" (page 33) he did not send to Dalziel for another seven months, writing to him from Bowerswell on 8 August 1859: "I send you a block of the unfortunate Virgins too late. It is very dark as it says midnight, the other of the Good Virgins which I am about will also be dark but not so much so. After these the others will be light—This will require most careful cutting like the Importunate Widow—the background should be cut to look a little lighter than it looks in the drawing, *greyer*. Be most careful to render the faces & keep the draperies rich & strong. I will now keep on giving you work—you will see these drawings are no joke as regards manipulation & design & understand how it is I cannot turn them out easily."

Millais was thoroughly depressed at this time. His two main pictures, on which he had laboured so hard the year before—"The Vale of Rest" and "Apple Blossom"—had been badly received. Although Ruskin in his *Academy Notes* owned that the first was "a great work," he also called it "frightful" in its ugliness. As for the other, after damning it thoroughly, he added, ". . .there is, I regret to say, no ground for any diminution of the doubt which I expressed two years since respecting the future career of a painter who can fall thus greatly beneath himself." "The Vale of Rest" remained unsold for several years and Millais had to do a great deal of repainting on the other before a dealer could be found to take it.

He believed his career was blasted, largely because of Ruskin's hostility; being of a very nervous temperament he was easily discouraged and Effie must have suffered a good deal from his despondency as well as from her own ill health. Her confinements were difficult and protracted and she took a long time to recover from them. Millais realised that nuns digging a grave was not a subject to appeal to the public, but nor, it seemed, was that of pretty girls lying in an apple orchard. How could he please them? He had in fact already found the subject for a winner in "The Black Brunswicker," a scene in a drawing-room in Brussels on the eve of Waterloo where an officer of this crack German regiment says goodbye to an English girl. As soon as he started work on this picture Millais's spirits revived and it was with renewed energy that he started again on the Parables.

In an undated letter from Bowerswell, presumably autumn 1859, he wrote, "I send off the Parable of the Leaven [page 7] which the woman hid in three measures of wheat. She is mixing the leaven in the last of the three—the girl at the back I have made near the oven with one of the loaves & the other rests against the wall of the window. I have another just finished of the Hidden Treasure and I am determined to be always at work upon them. It is almost unnecessary for me to say that I cannot produce them quickly even if supposing I gave *all my* time to them,—they are *separate pictures* & do I exert myself to the utmost I make them as complete as possible [*sic*]. I can do ordinary illustrations as quickly as most men, but these designs can scarcely be regarded in this same light— each Parable I illustrate perhaps a dozen times before I fix, and the hidden Treasure I have altered upon the wood at least *six* times. . . .I am also about the Parable of the Sower. I suppose you have nearly completed the 5 foolish Virgins. I am always anxious to get proofs." "The Sower" was not in fact the next one to be finished.

On 1 December, presumably 1859 still, he was writing from another furnished house in London, 1 Bryanston Place. In this letter he calls Dalziel by his name for the first time instead of writing "Dear Sir." "I have finished the Finding of the Treasure, & I will set about another immediately. . . . There is more white used in the last than I like but although comparatively simple its design has bothered me a great deal." There is certainly a great deal of white sky in "The Hidden Treasure" (page 13) without a cloud or even a bird in it.

In the next letter with no address but dated February 1860 he wrote, "The Parable is splendidly cut." This letter in the 1902 edition is placed before "The Lost Piece of Silver" which may have come after "The Hidden Treasure"; there was also another one finished before May 1860, probably "The Tares." By the time he wrote again he was assured of public acclaim for "The Black Brunswicker," although the critics, so accustomed now to deriding him, lagged behind in praise. One does not know Ruskin's opinion of this exquisitely painted though sentimental picture, for he stopped writing his *Academy Notes* after 1859. The main thing was that the picture was immediately sold for 1,000 pounds. Unfortunately the financial rewards of painting were becoming more and more important to Millais. Effie has sometimes been blamed for this, most unfairly unless she can be blamed for having too many children.

Back at Bowerswell after the opening of the Academy, with his picture sold, and four days after the birth of his second daughter and fourth child, he wrote on 17 May 1860: "I am just finishing the Pearl of great

Fig. 5. "The Good Samaritan": study for the composition, pen and sepia ink; 2¼ × 2 in. (British Museum)

Fig. 6. "The Good Samaritan": study for the donkey; pencil, pen and sepia ink, 6 × 3½ in. (British Museum)

Price [page 15]—a model is waiting at this *moment*—a *Donkey*, & I will send it off *tomorrow*." This same donkey with the same bell round its neck can be seen in "The Good Samaritan" (page 39).

But it was not for another four days that he sent off the block with a covering letter: "At last I have finished 'The Pearl of Great Price'—you will at once see there is a tremendous lot of work in it—& I have put a little more white in parts than perhaps is good,—but I could not help it as I require to alter a good deal—I know very well you will give it all your attention and after those that you have done I feel sure it will be rendered a facsimile. . . . I am about another this afternoon, & will try & do the next twenty as quickly as possible. I must repeat that such drawings are the work of *days*, & *weeks* of arrangement—I could do them all very quickly as you can guess, but not in that style."

A comparison of the illustration with the beautiful water-colour drawing (Fig. 3) shows the limitations of wood-engraving, even with the most expert cutting. This last letter tells us that "The Pearl of Great Price" was the tenth drawing Millais sent in and that it was still his intention to do thirty according to his original undertaking. It is not known at what stage the Dalziels released him from the last ten; we merely know from their book that ". . . he required us to release him from the remainder of the agreement, and to this we had no choice but to comply, though we did so very reluctantly, feeling that the world of art would be that much poorer."

The next letter, without an address, though probably written from Bowerswell, was dated 10 June 1860: "I send off another Parable, 'The Sower' [page 4]. I have made it chiefly landscape for variety, & to show the *stony* ground, Briars, nettles, & fowls of the air, feeding upon the stray seed. The Sower who is supposed to have sown the side of the field first is subordinate—The trees in the back I have left in pencil having drawn them from nature—I am afraid I should only confuse you by working ink over them—cut them as though drawn with the pen and they will come out then chief [*sic*] dark. All the stories etc will need most *careful* cutting as they are drawn, just as much care as *though they were faces*. . . Please cut the pigeons most carefully, as the drawing should be very tender." On 2 July 1860 he was writing again from Bowerswell to say he was "about the good Virgins."

There is a gap now of almost two years in Millais's letters to Dalziel. The next, though undated, is written from 7 Cromwell Place, South Kensington, and must, therefore, be 1862 as he did not move into this house, the first home of his own, until early that year. "I have now finished one

Fig. 7. "The Foolish Virgins": study, pencil drawing, 5¾ ×
4½ in. (Boston Museum of Fine Arts)

of the Parables & you shall have the other Lazarus immediately only wait a day—The one I send please cut with all your might, the subject is the *discontented labourers* ["The Labourers in the Vineyard," page 23]. I have used pencil in parts to soften—the vineyard at the back cannot be too delicately worked, the work on the figures shd be close & to have the effect it has in drawing—Oh!!!!!! what labour they are to me after the offhand business of late. As soon as the Lazarus is done I will set about the 'Lost Sheep' so you will have your work cut out."

The "offhand business" may have referred to a serial Millais was illustrating, *Mistress and Maid* by Dinah Mulock, which ran in *Good Words* throughout 1862. He was also still turning out illustrations for Trollope's *Orley Farm* which was published in monthly parts from March 1861 to October 1862. It is evident that he was exhausted by the Parables; the Dalziels must have had their patience almost exhausted too, though they were mollified no doubt by Millais's continued praise. In a letter which can be dated about March 1862 from references in it to other work he wrote, "The Parable wants a little [word omitted] but it is most beautifully rendered—indeed all the Parables are *perfection* of engraving on wood."

On 10 May 1862, he was writing again from Cromwell Place: "I am sorry I haven't finished Lazarus as I had hoped. I have worked at it ever since I last wrote but the dogs trouble me. All is finished but the background & next week you shall have the other the Shepherd & Sheep ["The Lost Sheep"]. . . . I think the last is about the best I have ever done. What a pity they have hung the Parable proofs so badly at the R.A. too high."

It is uncertain whether by "the last" Millais meant "The Lost Sheep" (page 53) or "The Rich Man and Lazarus" (page 65). The former is his most beautiful landscape; in the latter the head of Lazarus is certainly very fine but the curled white baluster is so obtrusive that it spoils the composition. The dog lying down in the foreground was Effie's beautiful deerhound, Roswell. Millais used it over and over again as a model, though he used it in only one other Parable—"The Pearl of Great Price." Its appearance of docility is deceptive, for after being with Effie for a number of years it had to be transported to Australia for poaching.

Not only was "The Lost Piece of Silver" (page 55) among the Parable proofs hung too high at the Academy, but this was the year in which the oil painting of the same subject, later destroyed in a gas explosion, was exhibited. A mezzotint of it shows that the composition was almost identical to that of the engraving. The *Art Journal* for June 1862 commented

Fig. 8. "The Pharisee and Publican": studies, pen and brown ink, 7¼ × 4½ in. (Boston Museum of Fine Arts)

on the painting: "The title, in its application to this picture, is simply absurd, the figure being a modern maid-servant, with a broom in one hand, and a brass candle-stick in the other, looking for something on the ground. The effect is, of course, that of candle-light, and, as a sketch, it might be attributed to Velasquez. We are, however, bound to accept it as a picture, and as a picture, its athletic dash reverses every maxim that has been enunciated as a precept of Pre-Raphaelitism."

Millais's next letter is not until October 1862: "Here at last is another Parable & another is in hand this week. The quality of the work speaks for itself and I need not tell you to cut it with all your might. . . . I have done the vine elaborately from nature for the next Parable the labourers in the Vineyard who kill the heir." This refers to "The Wicked Husband-men" (page 29). No one could have accused Millais of executing this drawing with "athletic dash." The vine and its tendrils could not have failed to delight Ruskin. The piece of rope round the heir's neck is a highly imaginative way of showing he has been murdered, and the dead bird and, particularly, the toad, bring a sense of evil to the scene. This drawing is perhaps more Pre-Raphaelite in feeling than any of the others, but it comes as rather a shock to recognise in this Eastern vineyard the identical wall of Balhousie Castle, Perth, which Millais used as a background for "The Love of James I of Scotland." (See Fig. 4.)

Another year was to go by before the twenty drawings were finished, and perhaps it was during that year, as the work dragged on, that the Dalziels released Millais from the other ten. At last he came to the penultimate one, writing on 8 September 1863, ten days before the birth of his fifth child: "I have just left off working on the Marriage Feast Parable which is now nearly finished. . . . I write this to ask which other Parable you wish for the last, as I wish to commence it & be done with the business altogether—In your old list there was the 'Good Shepherd' who sacrificed his life for the Sheep, and there is the 'Talents' [included in the book as "Ten Pieces of Money"] which would not make such a good illustration. I can think of no important Parable left undone."

It was evidently Millais's reference to "The Marriage of the King's Son" as "The Marriage Feast" that caused the confusion over this Parable, but that he intended to illustrate the former is shown by his mentioning when he received the proof that the "King's head was a little coarse in the shadow." There is no King in "The Marriage Feast"; in that Parable the host is simply described as "a certain man."

It is interesting to note that in "The Good Shepherd" (page 73) Millais, who usually followed the story so meticulously in his illustrations, drew

Fig. 9. "The Importunate Friend": original drawing on wood block in pen and ink on background of Chinese white, 5½ × 4¼ in. (Johannesburg Art Gallery)

a lion in place of a wolf. Was this because he had already given us a wolf in "The Tares" (page 9)? Yet the wolf in that picture is merely a background spectre in the night; one might have expected a more carefully drawn wolf for a prominent daylight role without thinking Millais had repeated himself. He was at Bowerswell when he made this drawing and there seems little doubt that against all his former Pre-Raphaelite principles he copied the lion from a book instead of taking the trouble to find a live wolf or even a live lion. There was no zoo in Edinburgh at that time but he had only to go to London to find a wolf or a lion. Can one regard this lion as a symbol of the lack of artistic integrity of which Millais was accused when once he found worldly success? In comparing the first drawing he made, "The Good Samaritan" (page 39), with "The Good Shepherd" does one see in the former the true Pre-Raphaelite and in the latter just another commercially successful artist? Or does the last drawing simply show an increased understanding of both the possibilities and limitations of the medium after six years of experience?

How much had happened in those six years, both in his personal and professional life; he had brought four children into the world and had passed from artistic uncertainty to assured success, culminating at about the same time as the Parable book was published in his election to full membership of the Royal Academy.

On 5 December 1863, he was able to write to Dalziel, "I am quite *delighted* with the Book, and I think you will find the public will slowly & surely appreciate it—Six copies will not quite do for the friends I have promised it to. . . . I desired to send copies to men who will forward the sale—such as Tennyson, Layard, Thackeray, Leech etc." Thackeray could have done little to forward the sale for he was dead by Christmas.

Although the book is dated 1864 it was published on 10 December 1863, and advertised in the *Bookseller* as "Dalziels' Christmas Book," with a quotation from the *Reader*: "In these designs we have much of Mr Millais' finest work, while Messrs. Dalziel have raised the character of Wood Engraving by their exact and most admirable translation." The title page bore the publisher's name, Routledge, Warne, and Routledge, Farrington Street, London. The price was a guinea. Some of the copies were bound in red, some in blue and some in green, but all were elaborately impressed with gold, while the paper was of the finest quality with red initial letters, headings and page lines. A few copies of the engravings only, on India paper, in a portfolio, were advertised at five guineas. Perhaps it was a mistake to bring the book out at Christmas time, for it seems to have been swamped with a spate of illustrated Christmas books,

Fig. 10. "The Good Shepherd": original drawing on wood block in pen and ink on background of Chinese white, 5½ × 4¼ in. (Johannesburg Art Gallery)

many of them of a religious character. In the words of the Dalziels themselves, the illustrations "did not receive that liberal recognition from
either the public or the critics which their undoubted excellence ought to
have commanded." The sales of the book were disappointing and it did
not go into a second edition.

There were very few reviews. The book was not noticed at all in *The
Times*, although for two weeks running that paper devoted several col-
umns to the Christmas publications. "The Pearl of Great Price" was
reproduced in the *Bookseller*, though not in reference to the book but in
a review of the complete volume of *Good Words* for 1863. *Good Words*
was the most successful illustrated monthly magazine of the time, with a
circulation of almost 100,000, so Millais must have been gratified when
the *Bookseller* stated that Guthrie's articles with Millais's twelve illustrations had been the chief feature of the magazine that year. In drawing
attention to "The Pearl of Great Price" the reviewer commented: "Mark
the earnestness of the different actors . . . the mixture of eagerness, curi-
osity and shrewdness displayed in the various faces, and the contempt
with which the fortunate finder refuses the proferred money." Others may
interpret this drawing differently and see not contempt in the finder's
face but distrust, an unwillingness to part with the pearl until he has
the money in his hands.

The book was reviewed twice in the *Art Journal* (February and April
1864). The first notice was short but as laudatory as Millais could have
wished. The second was very long and included reproductions of "The
Pearl of Great Price" and "The Unmerciful Servant." After discussing the
Pre-Raphaelite school in general terms it went on to describe and praise
the illustrations. "The Labourers in the Vineyard" was stated to be "one
of the most original compositions in the volume," and "The Good Samaritan" had never been "illustrated with more pathetic eloquence." It was
this second reviewer who pointed out that in "The Marriage Feast" there
was "a misquotation of the text with reference to the subject."

The most interesting review, however, was a very mixed one in the *Ath-
enaeum* (December 1863). High praise was given to the Dalziels' share in
the undertaking, and many of the designs were considered to possess
"high qualities of Art"; particularly noted were the strength of the
woman's hands in "The Leaven," the "noble composition" of "The
Unmerciful Servant" and the "Satanic force about the figure of the steal-
thy Enemy of mankind sowing tares at night." Millais was much criti-
cised, however, for not treating the work consistently as a whole. Two
courses had been open to him, it was argued, both "legitimate to Art"—

either to bring to his drawings a rich local colour, oriental costumes and accessories, knowledge and observation of Eastern customs unchanged since long before the days of Our Lord (it was even suggested that he might have done well to take a trip to the Holy Land)—or else to make them uniformly modern in feeling, an approach which need not have led him to the extreme of dressing the ten virgins in crinolines.

There is something to be said for this criticism; one does get the impression that Millais never troubled to study the hidden meaning or symbolism of the Parables as he might well have done by simply reading Archbishop Trench's book on the subject. Without an understanding of the ancient customs of the East many of the Parables remain obscure and seem inexplicably cruel. Millais evidently read the stories as carefully as he read Trollope (it was his fidelity to the story line that so delighted Trollope) but never attempted to penetrate their mysteries. For the most part he was content to give them authentic Scottish backgrounds—Scottish trees and thistles, Scottish cows, donkeys and castle walls. Could anything be less like the pariah dogs of the East than the domestic pets licking the sores of Lazarus?

Only in "The Pharisee and Publican" and, more vaguely, in "The Unjust Judge" and "The Pearl of Great Price" did he attempt an oriental realism, and for these one rather suspects he may have borrowed sketches from Holman Hunt, who had spent years in the Holy Land in search of verisimilitude for his religious work.

Yet, when all this has been said, surely it is the very variety of Millais's treatment of his subjects and their unequalness that give them so much charm. How delightful it is suddenly to come across a Renaissance church in the background of "The Unmerciful Servant" (St Paul's?) and find the wicked husbandmen standing in the doorway of Balhousie Castle. And would not one rather have a vine copied from the greenhouse at Bowerswell, "fowls of the air" from the family dovecote, the childrens' donkey brought to the stable yard, loaves kneaded by the Grays' cook, and a deerhound that might that very morning have been chasing the lost sheep or might even have just killed the sheep for which the shepherd gave his life (perhaps this was the very act for which Roswell was sentenced to transportation: he does not appear in any drawing after 1863)—would not one rather have all this domestic realism than a uniformity of oriental detail that could only have come from books?

How many times did Effie and her sisters pose for the ten virgins? And was not the same dress used for them all—a dress no doubt run up by Effie herself who was an expert needlewoman? Only one virgin is slightly differentiated from the others in both illustrations by the beads round her neck. Isn't the woman's skirt in "The Leaven" the same as that of the serving wench in "Lazarus," hitched up by Effie's needle? Does not the Sower have round his neck the same bag as the Evil One sowing tares? Has not the same cloak been made to do for "The Unmerciful Servant," "The Labourers in the Vineyard," "The Wicked Husbandmen" and "The Marriage Feast"? Is not the widow pleading with the Judge wearing the same gown as the girl looking for the lost piece of silver? And surely the Publican had borrowed his robe from the father of the Prodigal Son? No doubt a careful comparison of the faces would also reveal that the male models had played many different roles throughout the book. And would we have it otherwise? This may not be the correct approach to art but surely such details endear the illustrations to us the more we observe them.

There is, of course, a danger that a knowledge of Millais's mood and circumstances at the time he executed each drawing may prejudice one in favour of some more than others. Thus, the realisation that he wanted "to be done with the business altogether" may account for the fact that "The Good Shepherd," in spite of the great understanding it shows of the engraver's art, seems so sterile. And does one sense in "The Foolish Virgins" some of the artist's own depression at the bad reception of his 1859 Academy pictures? Is it only imagination that sees his love for Effie reflected in the tender expression of the girl looking for the lost coin, or senses some of the ebullience and vitality in "The Good Samaritan" and "The Prodigal Son" with which Millais started off on the project, fully intending to produce thirty drawings in as many weeks? And is not the strength that emanates from "The Pearl of Great Price" directly attributable to Millais's renewed confidence after the success of "The Black Brunswicker"?

These rather irreverent considerations should not detract from Millais's true artistic achievement in these illustrations. One can only wish that he had been prevailed upon to produce the other ten, and feel with the Dalziels that the world of art is poorer without them.

— Mary Lutyens

London, 1974

SELECT BIBLIOGRAPHY

Academy Notes (*The Complete Works of John Ruskin,* edited by Cook and Wedderburn, Vol. XIV: London, 1904).

Boston Museum Bulletin, Vol. LXXI, 1973: *The Hartley Collection of Victorian Illustration* by Sarah Hamilton Phelps.

The Brothers Dalziel. A Record of Fifty Years' Work in Conjunction with Many of the Most Distinguished Artists of the Period 1840–1890 (London, 1901).

Catalogue for the 1967 Millais Exhibition at the Royal Academy and the Walker Art Gallery Liverpool by Mary Bennett.

Good Words (London, 1863).

The Life and Letters of Sir John Everett Millais by J. G. Millais (London, 1899).

Liverpool Bulletin, Walker Art Gallery 1967: *Footnote to the Millais Exhibition* by Mary Bennett.

Millais and the Ruskins by Mary Lutyens (London, 1967).

Notes on the Parables by Richard Chevenix Trench, D.D. (London, 1841).

Phototransference of Drawings in Wood-block Engravings by Sir Paul Fildes (*Journal of the Printing Historical Society,* Number 5, 1969).

Poems of Alfred Tennyson, illustrated by T. Creswick, J. E. Millais, W. Mulready, D. Maclise, Clarkson Stanfield, J. C. Horsley, etc. (London, 1857).

Twenty India Paper Proofs of the Drawings of Sir J. E. Millais with Which is Given a Collection of Twenty Autograph Letters (in Facsimile) from Millais to the Dalziels during the Progress of the Work (privately printed London, 1902). Less than fifty copies were printed.

Walpole Society Journal, 1972–1974: *Letters from Sir John Everett Millais, Bart, P.R.A.* in the Huntington Library, San Marino, California, edited by Mary Lutyens.

LOCATION OF MILLAIS'S PAINTINGS MENTIONED IN TEXT

"Apple Blossom" (Viscount Leverhulme)

"The Black Brunswicker" (Lady Lever Art Gallery, Port Sunlight, near Liverpool)

"The Love of James I of Scotland" (untraced)

"Sir Isumbras at the Ford" (Lady Lever Art Gallery)

"The Tares" (Birmingham Art Gallery)

"The Vale of Rest" (Tate Gallery)

LOCATION OF WATER-COLOUR
DRAWINGS OF PARABLES

THE FOGG ART MUSEUM,
CAMBRIDGE, MASS.
  "The Lost Piece of Silver"
  "The Good Samaritan"
  "The Labourers in the Vineyard"
  "The Foolish Virgins"
  "The Rich Man and Lazarus"
  "The Unjust Judge"

WHITWORTH ART GALLERY,
MANCHESTER
  "The Foolish Virgins"
  "The Tares"

ABERDEEN ART GALLERY
  "The Hidden Treasure"
  "The Leaven"
  "The Pharisee and Publican"

BRITISH MUSEUM
  "The Pearl of Great Price"

THE PARABLES

OF

WITH PICTURES BY

JOHN EVERETT MILLAIS.

ENGRAVED BY

THE BROTHERS DALZIEL.

LONDON

ROUTLEDGE, WARNE, AND ROUTLEDGE,
FARRINGDON STREET.
1864.

PREFACE.

Mr. Millais made his firſt drawing to illuſtrate the Parables in August, 1857, and the laſt in October, 1863. Thus he has been able to give that care and conſideration to his ſubjects, which the beauty as well as the importance of " The Parables" demanded ; for the work has extended over a period of ſix years.

The Brothers Dalziel have ſeconded his efforts with all earneſtneſs, deſiring, as far as their power would go, to make the Pictures ſpecimens of the art of wood engraving.

London,
    December, 1863.

"And He spake
many things unto them
in Parables."

The Parable of the Sower.

BEHOLD, a fower went forth to fow;
And when he fowed, fome feeds fell by the way
fide, and the fowls came and devoured them up :

Some fell upon ftony places, where they had not much
earth : and forthwith they fprung up, becaufe they had no
deepnefs of earth :

And when the fun was up, they were fcorched ; and
becaufe they had no root, they withered away.

And fome fell among thorns ; and the thorns fprung up,
and choked them :

But other fell into good ground, and brought forth fruit,
fome an hundredfold, fome fixtyfold, fome thirtyfold.

Who hath ears to hear, let him hear.

.   .   .   .   .

Hear ye therefore the parable of the fower.

When any one heareth the word of the kingdom, and
underftandeth it not, then cometh the wicked one, and
catcheth away that which was fown in his heart. This is he
which received feed by the way fide.

The Sower.

But he that received the feed into ftony places, the fame is he that heareth the word, and anon with joy receiveth it;

Yet hath he not root in himfelf, but dureth for a while: for when tribulation or perfecution arifeth becaufe of the word, by-and-by he is offended.

He alfo that received feed among the thorns is he that heareth the word; and the care of this world, and the deceitfulnefs of riches, choke the word, and he becometh unfruitful.

But he that received feed into the good ground is he that heareth the word, and underftandeth it; which alfo
beareth fruit, and bringeth forth,
fome an hundredfold, fome
fixty, fome thirty.

Matthew, Chap. xiii.
v. iii.—xxiii.

The Parable of the Leaven.

THE kingdom of heaven is like unto leaven, which a woman took, and hid in three meafures of meal, till the whole was leavened.

Matthew, Chap. xiii.
v. xxxiii.

The Leaven.

The Parable of the Tares.

THE kingdom of heaven is likened unto a man which fowed good feed in his field:

But while men flept, his enemy came and fowed tares among the wheat, and went his way.

But when the blade was fprung up, and brought forth fruit, then appeared the tares alfo.

So the fervants of the houfeholder came and faid unto him, Sir, didft not thou fow good feed in thy field? from whence then hath it tares?

He faid unto them, An enemy hath done this. The fervants faid unto him, Wilt thou then that we go and gather them up?

But he faid, Nay; left while ye gather up the tares, ye root up alfo the wheat with them.

Let both grow together until the harveft: and in the time of harveft I will fay to the reapers, Gather ye together firft the tares, and bind them in bundles to burn them: but gather the wheat into my barn.

Matthew, Chap. xiii.
v. xxiv.—xxx.

8

The Tares.

The Parable of the Mustard Seed.

THE kingdom of heaven is like to a grain of muſtard ſeed, which a man took, and ſowed in his field:
Which indeed is the leaſt of all ſeeds: but when it is grown, it is the greateſt among herbs, and becometh a tree, ſo that the birds of the air come and lodge in the branches thereof.

Matthew, Chap. xiii.
v. xxxi., xxxii.

The Parable of the Hidden Treasure.

HE kingdom of heaven is like unto treaſure hid in a field; the which when a man hath found, he hideth, and for joy thereof goeth and ſelleth all that he hath, and buyeth that field.

Matthew, Chap. xiii.
v. xliv.

The Hidden Treasure.

The Parable of the Pearl of Great Price.

THE kingdom of heaven is like unto a merchant man,
ſeeking goodly pearls:
Who, when he had found one pearl of great price,
went and ſold all that he had,
and bought it.

Matthew, Chap. xiii.
v. xlv., xlvi.

14

The Pearl of Great Price.

The Parable of the Draw-net.

THE kingdom of heaven is like unto a net, that was caſt into the ſea, and gathered of every kind:

Which, when it was full, they drew to ſhore, and ſat down, and gathered the good into veſſels, but caſt the bad away.

So ſhall it be at the end of the world: the angels ſhall come forth, and ſever the wicked from among the juſt,

And ſhall caſt them into the furnace of fire: there ſhall be wailing and gnaſhing of teeth.

Matthew, Chap. xiii.
v. xlvii.—l.

The Parable of the Unmerciful Servant.

THEREFORE is the kingdom of heaven likened unto a certain king, which would take account of his fervants.

And when he had begun to reckon, one was brought unto him, which owed him ten thoufand talents.

But forafmuch as he had not to pay, his lord commanded him to be fold, and his wife, and children, and all that he had, and payment to be made.

The fervant therefore fell down, and worfhipped him, faying, Lord, have patience with me, and I will pay thee all.

Then the lord of that fervant was moved with compaffion, and loofed him, and forgave him the debt.

But the fame fervant went out, and found one of his fellowfervants, which owed him an hundred pence : and he laid hands on him, and took him by the throat, faying, Pay me that thou oweft.

And his fellowfervant fell down at his feet, and befought him, faying, Have patience with me, and I will pay thee all.

The Unmerciful Servant.

And he would not : but went and caſt him into priſon, till he ſhould pay the debt.

So when his fellowſervants ſaw what was done, they were very ſorry, and came and told unto their lord all that was done.

Then his lord, after that he had called him, ſaid unto him, O thou wicked ſervant, I forgave thee all that debt, becauſe thou deſiredſt me :

Shouldeſt not thou alſo have had compaſſion on thy fellowſervant, even as I had pity on thee ?

And his lord was wroth, and delivered him to the tormentors, till he ſhould pay all that was due unto him.

So likewiſe ſhall my heavenly Father do alſo unto you, if ye from your hearts forgive not every one his brother their treſpaſſes.

Matthew, Chap. xviii.

v. xxiii.—xxxv.

The Parable of the Labourers in the Vineyard.

FOR the kingdom of heaven is like unto a man that is an houſeholder, which went out early in the morning to hire labourers into his vineyard.

And when he had agreed with the labourers for a penny a day, he ſent them into his vineyard.

And he went out about the third hour, and ſaw others ſtanding idle in the market-place.

And ſaid unto them; Go ye alſo into the vineyard, and whatſoever is right I will give you. And they went their way.

Again he went out about the ſixth and ninth hour, and did likewiſe.

And about the eleventh hour he went out, and found others ſtanding idle, and ſaith unto them, Why ſtand ye here all the day idle?

They ſay unto him, Becauſe no man hath hired us. He ſaith unto them, Go ye alſo into the vineyard; and whatſoever is right, that ſhall ye receive.

So when even was come, the lord of the vineyard ſaith

The Labourers of the Vineyard.

unto his steward, Call the labourers and give them their hire, beginning from the last unto the first.

And when they came that were hired about the eleventh hour, they received every man a penny.

But when the first came, they supposed that they should have received more; and they likewise received every man a penny.

And when they had received it, they murmured against the goodman of the house,

Saying, These last have wrought but one hour, and thou hast made them equal unto us, which have borne the burden and heat of the day.

But he answered one of them, and said, Friend, I do thee no wrong : didst not thou agree with me for a penny?

Take that thine is, and go thy way : I will give unto this last, even as unto thee.

Is it not lawful for me to do what I will with mine own? Is thine eye evil, because I am good?

So the last shall be first, and the first last : for many be called, but few chosen.

Matthew, Chap. xx.
v. i.—xvi.

The Parable of the Two Sons.

BUT what think ye? A certain man had two fons; and he came to the firft, and faid, Son, go work to day in my vineyard.

He anfwered and faid, I will not: but afterward he repented, and went.

And he came to the fecond, and faid likewife. And he anfwered and faid, I go, fir: and went not.

Whether of them twain did the will of his father? They fay unto him, The first. Jefus faith unto them, Verily I fay unto you, That the Publicans and the harlots go into the kingdom of God before you.

For John came unto you in the way of righteoufnefs, and ye believed him not: but the Publicans and the harlots believed him: and ye, when ye had feen it, repented not afterward, that ye might believe him.

Matthew, Chap. xxi
v. xxviii.—xxxii.

25

The Parable of the Wicked Husbandmen.

THERE was a certain houſeholder, which planted a vineyard, and hedged it round about, and digged a wineprefs in it, and built a tower, and let it out to huſband-men, and went into a far country:

And when the time of the fruit drew near, he ſent his ſervants to the huſbandmen, that they might receive the fruits of it.

And the huſbandmen took his ſervants, and beat one, and killed another, and ſtoned another.

Again, he ſent other ſervants more than the firſt: and they did unto them likewiſe.

But laſt of all he ſent unto them his ſon, ſaying, They will reverence my ſon.

But when the huſbandmen ſaw the ſon, they ſaid among themſelves, This is the heir; come, let us kill him, and let us ſeize on his inheritance.

And they caught him, and caſt him out of the vineyard, and flew him.

When the lord therefore of the vineyard cometh, what will he do unto thofe hufbandmen?

They fay unto him, He will miferably deftroy thofe wicked men, and will let out his vineyard unto other hufbandmen, which fhall render him the fruits in their feafons.

Jefus faith unto them, Did ye never read in the Scriptures, The ftone which the builders rejected, the fame is become the head of the corner: this is the Lord's doing, and it is marvellous in our eyes?

Therefore fay I unto you, The kingdom of God fhall be taken from you, and given to a nation bringing forth the fruits thereof.

And whofoever fhall fall on this ftone fhall be broken: but on whomfoever it fhall fall, it will grind him to powder.

Matthew, Chap. xxi.
v. xxxiii.—xliv.

The Wicked Huſbandmen.

The Parable of the Ten Virgins.

THEN ſhall the kingdom of heaven be likened unto ten virgins, which took their lamps, and went forth to meet the bridegroom.

And five of them were wiſe, and five were fooliſh.

They that were fooliſh took their lamps, and took no oil with them :

But the wiſe took oil in their veſſels with their lamps.

While the bridegroom tarried, they all ſlumbered and ſlept.

And at midnight there was a cry made, Behold, the bridegroom cometh ; go ye out to meet him.

Then all thoſe virgins aroſe, and trimmed their lamps.

And the fooliſh ſaid unto the wiſe, Give us of your oil ; for our lamps are gone out.

But the wiſe anſwered, ſaying, Not ſo ; leſt there be not enough for us and you : but go ye rather to them that ſell, and buy for yourſelves.

The Wife and Foolish Virgins.

And while they went to buy, the bridegroom came ; and they that were ready went in with him to the marriage : and the door was ſhut.

Afterward came alſo the other virgins, ſaying, Lord, Lord, open to us.

But he anſwered and ſaid, Verily I ſay unto you, I know you not.

Watch therefore, for ye know neither the day nor the hour wherein the Son of man cometh.

Matthew, Chap. xxv.
v. i.—xiii.

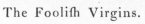

The Foolish Virgins.

The Parable of the Seed Growing Secretly.

SO is the kingdom of God, as if a man fhould caft feed into the ground;

And fhould fleep, and rife night and day, and the feed fhould fpring and grow up, he knoweth not how.

For the earth bringeth forth fruit of herfelf; firft the blade, then the ear, after that the full corn in the ear.

But when the fruit is brought forth, immediately
he putteth in the fickle, becaufe
the harveft is come.

Mark, Chap. iv
v. xxvi.—xxix.

The Parable of the Fig Tree.

NOW learn a parable of the fig tree ; When her branch is yet tender, and putteth forth leaves, ye know that summer is near :

So ye in like manner, when ye ſhall ſee theſe things come to paſs, know that it is nigh, even at the doors.

Verily I ſay unto you, that this generation ſhall not paſs, till all theſe things be done.

*Heaven and earth ſhall paſs away : but my words
ſhall not paſs away.*

Mark, Chap. xiii.
v. xxviii.—xxxi.

35

The Parable of the Merciful Creditor.

THERE was a certain creditor which had two debtors : the one owed five hundred pence, and the other fifty.

And when they had nothing to pay, he frankly forgave them both. Tell me therefore, which of them will love him moſt ?

Simon anſwered and ſaid, I ſuppoſe that he, to whom he forgave moſt. And he ſaid unto him, Thou haſt rightly judged.

And he turned to the woman, and ſaid unto Simon, Seeſt thou this woman ? I entered into thine houſe, thou gaveſt me no water for my feet : but ſhe hath waſhed my feet with tears, and wiped them with the hairs of her head.

Thou gaveſt me no kiſs : but this woman ſince the time I came in hath not ceaſed to kiſs my feet.

My head with oil thou didſt not anoint : but this woman hath anointed my feet with ointment.

Wherefore I ſay unto thee, Her ſins, which are many, are forgiven ; for ſhe loved much : but to whom little is forgiven, the ſame loveth little.

Luke, Chap. vii.
v. xli.—xlvii.

The Parable of the Good Samaritan.

A CERTAIN man went down from Jeruſalem to Jericho, and fell among thieves, which ſtripped him of his raiment, and wounded him, and departed, leaving him half dead.

And by chance there came down a certain Prieſt that way : and when he ſaw him, he paſſed by on the other ſide.

And likewiſe a Levite, when he was at the place, came and looked on him, and paſſed by on the other ſide.

But a certain Samaritan, as he journeyed, came where he was : and when he ſaw him, he had compaſſion on him,

And went to him, and bound up his wounds, pouring in oil and wine, and ſet him on his own beaſt, and brought him to an inn, and took care of him.

And on the morrow when he departed, he took out two-pence, and gave them to the hoſt, and ſaid unto him, Take care of him ; and whatſoever thou ſpendeſt more, when I come again, I will repay thee.

Which now of theſe three, thinkeſt thou, was neighbour unto him that fell among the thieves?

And he ſaid, He that ſhewed mercy on him. Then ſaid Jeſus unto him, Go, and do thou likewiſe.

Luke, Chap. x.
v. xxx.— xxxvii

38

The Good Samaritan.

The Parable of the Importunate Friend.

WHICH of you ſhall have a friend, and ſhall go unto him at midnight, and ſay unto him, Friend, lend me three loaves;

For a friend of mine in his journey is come to me, and I have nothing to ſet before him?

And he from within ſhall anſwer and ſay, Trouble me not: the door is now ſhut, and my children are with me in bed; I cannot riſe and give thee.

I ſay unto you, Though he will not riſe and give him, becauſe he is his friend, yet becauſe of his importunity he will riſe and give him as many as he needeth.

And I ſay unto you, Aſk, and it ſhall be given you; ſeek, and ye ſhall find; knock, and it ſhall be opened unto you.

For every one that aſketh receiveth; and he that ſeeketh findeth; and to him that knocketh it ſhall be opened.

The Importunate Friend.

If a ſon ſhall aſk bread of any of you that is a father, will he give him a ſtone? or if he aſk a fiſh, will he for a fiſh give him a ſerpent?

Or if he ſhall aſk an egg, will he offer him a ſcorpion?

If ye then, being evil, know how to give good gifts unto your children: how much more ſhall your heavenly Father give the Holy Spirit to them that aſk him?

Luke, Chap. xi.
v. v.—xiii.

The Parable of the Rich Man.

THE ground of a certain rich man brought forth plentifully:

And he thought within himſelf, ſaying, What ſhall I do, becauſe I have no room where to beſtow my fruits?

And he ſaid, This will I do: I will pull down my barns, and build greater; and there will I beſtow all my fruits and my goods.

And I will ſay to my ſoul, Soul, thou haſt much goods laid up for many years; take thine eaſe, eat, drink, and be merry.

But God ſaid unto him, Thou fool, this night thy ſoul ſhall be required of thee: then whoſe ſhall thoſe things be, which thou haſt provided?

So is he that layeth up treaſure for himſelf, and is not rich toward God.

Luke, Chap. xii.
v. xvi.—xxi.

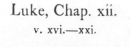

The Parable of the Faithful and Wicked Stewards.

WHO then is that faithful and wife fteward, whom his lord fhall make ruler over his houfehold, to give them their portion of meat in due feafon?

Bleffed is that fervant, whom his lord when he cometh fhall find fo doing.

Of a truth I fay unto you, that he will make him ruler over all that he hath.

But and if that fervant fay in his heart, My lord delayeth his coming; and fhall begin to beat the menfervants and maidens, and to eat and drink, and to be drunken;

The lord of that fervant will come in a day when he looketh not for him, and at an hour when he is not aware, and will cut him in funder, and will appoint him his portion with the unbelievers.

And that fervant, which knew his lord's will, and prepared not himfelf, neither did according to his will, fhall be beaten with many ftripes.

But he that knew not, and did commit things worthy
of ſtripes, ſhall be beaten with few ſtripes.

For unto whomſoever much is given, of him
ſhall be much required : and to whom
men have committed much, of him
they will aſk the more.

Luke, Chap. xii.
v. xlii.—xlviii.

The Parable of the Barren Fig Tree.

A CERTAIN man had a fig tree planted in his vine-yard; and he came and fought fruit thereon, and found none.

Then faid he unto the dreffer of his vineyard, Behold, thefe three years I come feeking fruit on this fig tree, and find none: cut it down; why cumbereth it the ground?

And he anfwering faid unto him, Lord, let it alone this year alfo, till I fhall dig about it, and dung it:

And if it bear fruit, well: and if not, then after that thou fhalt cut it down.

Luke, Chap. xiii.
v. vi.—ix.

46

The Parable of the Wedding Feast.

WHEN thou art bidden of any man to a wedding, fit not down in the higheft room; left a more honourable man than thou be bidden of him;

And he that bade thee and him come and fay to thee, Give this man place; and thou begin with fhame to take the loweft room.

But when thou art bidden, go and fit down in the loweft room; that when he that bade thee cometh, he may fay unto thee, Friend, go up higher: then fhalt thou have worfhip in the prefence of them that fit at meat with thee.

For whofoever exalteth himfelf fhall be abafed; and he that humbleth himfelf fhall be exalted.

Luke, Chap. xiv.
v. viii.—xi.

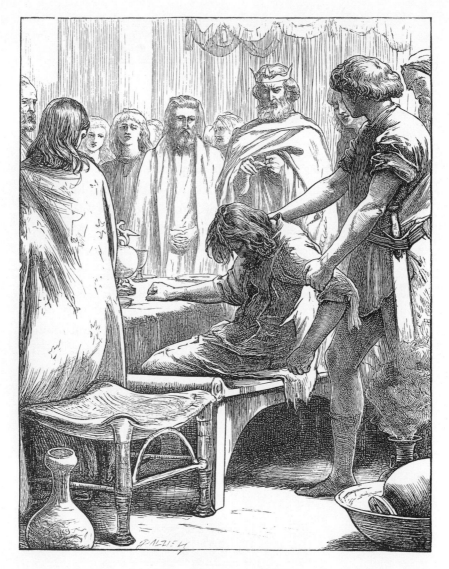

The Marriage Feaſt.

The Parable of the Marriage of the King's Son.

THE kingdom of heaven is like unto a certain king, which made a marriage for his fon,

And fent forth his fervants to call them that were bidden to the wedding: and they would not come.

Again, he fent forth other fervants, faying, Tell them which are bidden, Behold, I have prepared my dinner: my oxen and my fatlings are killed, and all things are ready: come unto the marriage.

But they made light of it, and went their ways, one to his farm, another to his merchandife:

And the remnant took his fervants, and entreated them fpitefully, and flew them.

But when the king heard thereof, he was wroth: and he fent forth his armies, and deftroyed thofe murderers, and burned up their city.

Then faith he to his fervants, The wedding is ready, but they which were bidden were not worthy.

Go ye therefore into the highways, and as many as ye fhall find, bid to the marriage.

So thofe fervants went out into the highways, and gathered together all as many as they found, both bad and good : and the wedding was furnifhed with guefts.

And when the king came in to fee the guefts, he faw a man which had not on a wedding garment :

And he faith unto him, Friend, how cameft thou in hither not having a wedding garment? And he was fpeechlefs.

Then faid the king to the fervants, Bind him hand and foot, and take him away, and caft him into outer darknefs ; there fhall be weeping and gnafhing of teeth.

For many are called, but few are chofen.

Matthew, Chap. xxii.
v. ii.—xiv.

The Parable of Perseverance.

FOR which of you, intending to build a tower, fitteth not down firft, and counteth the coft, whether he have fufficient to finifh it?

Left haply, after he hath laid the foundation, and is not able to finifh it, all that behold it begin to mock him,

Saying, This man began to build, and was not able to finifh.

Or what king, going to make war againft another king, fitteth not down firft, and confulteth whether he be able with ten thoufand to meet him that cometh againft him with twenty thoufand?

Or elfe, while the other is yet a great way off, he fendeth an ambaffage, and defireth conditions of peace.

So likewife, whofoever he be of you that forfaketh not all that he hath, he cannot be my difciple.

Luke, Chap. xiv.
v. xxviii.— xxxiii.

The Parable of the Lost Sheep.

WHAT man of you, having an hundred fheep, if he lofe one of them, doth not leave the ninety and nine in the wildernefs, and go after that which is loft, until he find it?

And when he hath found it, he layeth it on his fhoulders, rejoicing.

And when he cometh home, he calleth together his friends and neighbours, faying unto them, Rejoice with me; for I have found my fheep which was loft.

I fay unto you, that likewife joy fhall be in heaven
over one finner that repenteth, more than
over ninety and nine juft perfons,
which need no repentance.

Luke, Chap. xv.
v. iv.—vii.

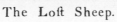

The Loſt Sheep.

The Parable of the Lost Piece of Silver.

EITHER what woman having ten pieces of filver, if fhe lofe one piece, doth not light a candle, and fweep the houfe, and feek diligently till fhe find it?

And when fhe hath found it, fhe calleth her friends and her neighbours together, faying, Rejoice with me; for I have found the piece which I had loft.

Likewife, I fay unto you, there is joy in the
prefence of the angels of God over
one finner that repenteth.

Luke, Chap. xv
v. viii.—x.

The Lost Piece of Silver.

The Parable of the Prodigal Son.

A CERTAIN man had two fons :
And the younger of them faid to his father,
Father, give me the portion of goods that falleth to me.
And he divided unto them his living.

And not many days after, the younger fon gathered all
together, and took his journey into a far country, and there
wafted his fubftance with riotous living.

And when he had fpent all, there arofe a mighty famine
in that land ; and he began to be in want.

And he went and joined himfelf to a citizen of that
country ; and he fent him into his fields to feed fwine.

And he would fain have filled his belly with the hufks
that the fwine did eat : and no man gave unto him.

And when he came to himfelf, he faid, How many hired
fervants of my father's have bread enough and to fpare, and
I perifh with hunger !

I will arife and go to my father, and will fay unto him,
Father I have finned againft heaven, and before thee,

The Prodigal Son.

And am no more worthy to be called thy fon : make me as one of thy hired fervants.

And he arofe, and came to his father. But when he was yet a great way off, his father faw him, and had compaffion, and ran, and fell on his neck, and kiffed him.

And the fon faid unto him, Father, I have finned againft heaven, and in thy fight, and am no more worthy to be called thy fon.

But the father faid to his fervants, Bring forth the beft robe, and put it on him ; and put a ring on his hand, and fhoes on his feet :

And bring hither the fatted calf, and kill it ; and let us eat, and be merry :

For this my fon was dead, and is alive again ; he was loft, and is found. And they began to be merry.

Now his elder fon was in the field : and as he came and drew nigh to the houfe, he heard musick and dancing.

And he called one of the fervants, and afked what thefe things meant.

And he faid unto him, Thy brother is come ; and thy father hath killed the fatted calf, becaufe he hath received him fafe and found.

And he was angry, and would not go in : therefore came his father out, and intreated him.

And he anfwering faid to his father, Lo, thefe many years do I ferve thee, neither tranfgreffed I at any time thy commandment : and yet thou never gaveſt me a kid, that I might make merry with my friends :

But as ſoon as this thy ſon was come, which hath devoured thy living with harlots, thou haſt killed for him the fatted calf.

And he ſaid unto him, Son, thou art ever with me, and all that I have is thine.

It was meet that we ſhould make merry, and be glad :
for this thy brother was dead, and is alive again ;
and was loſt, and is found.

Luke, Chap. xv.
v. xi. xxxii.

The Parable of the Unjust Steward.

THERE was a certain rich man, which had a steward; and the same was accused unto him that he had wasted his goods.

And he called him, and said unto him, How is it that I hear this of thee? give an account of thy stewardship; for thou mayest be no longer steward.

Then the steward said within himself, What shall I do? for my lord taketh away from me the stewardship: I cannot dig; to beg I am ashamed.

I am resolved what to do, that, when I am put out of the stewardship, they may receive me into their houses.

So he called every one of his lord's debtors unto him, and said unto the first, How much owest thou unto my lord?

And he said, An hundred measures of oil. And he said unto him, Take thy bill, and sit down quickly, and write fifty.

Then said he to another, And how much owest thou? And he said, An hundred measures of wheat. And he said unto him, Take thy bill, and write fourscore.

And the lord commended the unjuſt ſteward, becauſe he had done wiſely : for the children of this world are in their generation wiſer than the children of light.

And I ſay unto you, Make to yourſelves friends of the mammon of unrighteouſneſs ; that, when ye fail, they may receive you into everlaſting habitations.

He that is faithful in that which is leaſt is faithful alſo in much : and he that is unjuſt in the leaſt is unjuſt alſo in much.

If therefore ye have not been faithful in the unrighteous mammon, who will commit to your truſt the true riches .

And if ye have not been faithful in that which is another man's, who ſhall give you that which is your own ?

Luke, Chap. xvi.
v. i.—xii.

The Parable of the Rich Man and Lazarus.

THERE was a certain rich man, which was clothed in purple and fine linen, and fared fumptuoufly every day :

And there was a certain beggar named Lazarus, which was laid at his gate, full of fores,

And defiring to be fed with the crumbs which fell from the rich man's table : moreover the dogs came and licked his fores.

And it came to pafs, that the beggar died, and was carried by the angels into Abraham's bofom : the rich man alfo died, and was buried ;

And in hell he lift up his eyes, being in torments, and feeth Abraham afar off, and Lazarus in his bofom.

And he cried and faid, Father Abraham, have mercy on me, and fend Lazarus, that he may dip the tip of his finger in water, and cool my tongue ; for I am tormented in this flame.

But Abraham faid, Son, remember that thou in thy life-time receivedft thy good things, and likewife Lazarus evil things : but now he is comforted, and thou art tormented.

And befide all this, between us and you there is a great gulf fixed: fo that they which would pafs from hence to you cannot; neither can they pafs to us, that would come from thence.

Then he faid, I pray thee therefore, father, that thou wouldeft fend him to my father's houfe:

For I have five brethren; that he may teftify unto them, left they alfo come into this place of torment.

Abraham faith unto him, They have Mofes and the prophets; let them hear them.

And he faid, Nay, father Abraham: but if one went unto them from the dead, they will repent.

And he faid unto him, If they hear not Mofes and
the prophets, neither will they be
perfuaded, though one rofe
from the dead.

Luke, Chap. xvi.
v. xix.—xxxi.

The Rich Man and Lazarus.

The Parable of the Unjust Judge.

THERE was in a city a judge, which feared not God, neither regarded man:

And there was a widow in that city; and fhe came unto him, faying, Avenge me of mine adverfary.

And he would not for awhile: but afterward he faid within himfelf, Though I fear not God, nor regard man;

Yet becaufe this widow troubleth me, I will avenge her, left by her continual coming fhe weary me.

And the Lord faid, Hear what the unjuft judge faith.

And fhall not God avenge his own elect, which cry day and night unto him, though he bear long with them?

I tell you that he will avenge them fpeedily.   Neverthelefs when the Son of man cometh, fhall he find faith on the earth?

Luke, Chap. xviii.

v. ii.—viii.

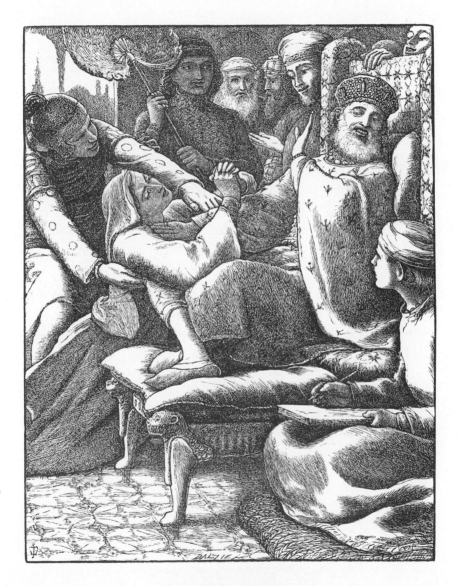

The Unjuſt Judge.

The Parable of the Pharisee and Publican.

TWO men went up into the temple to pray; the one a Pharifee, and the other a Publican.

The Pharifee ftood and prayed thus with himfelf, God, I thank thee, that I am not as other men are, extortioners, unjuft, adulterers, or even as this Publican.

I faft twice in the week, I give tithes of all that I poffefs.

And the Publican, ftanding afar off, would not lift up fo much as his eyes unto heaven, but fmote upon his breaft, faying, God be merciful to me a finner.

I tell you, this man went down to his houfe juftified rather than the other:

For every one that exalteth himfelf fhall be abafed;
and he that humbleth himfelf
fhall be exalted.

Luke, Chap. xviii.
v. x.—xiv.

The Pharisee and the Publican.

The Parable of the Ten Pieces of Money.

CERTAIN nobleman went into a far country to receive for himſelf a kingdom, and to return.

And he called his ten ſervants, and delivered them ten pounds, and ſaid unto them, Occupy till I come.

But his citizens hated him, and ſent a meſſage after him, ſaying, We will not have this man to reign over us.

And it came to paſs, that when he was returned, having received the kingdom, then he commanded theſe ſervants to be called unto him, to whom he had given the money, that he might know how much every man had gained by trading.

Then came the firſt, ſaying, Lord, thy pound hath gained ten pounds.

And he ſaid unto him, Well, thou good ſervant : becauſe thou haſt been faithful in a very little, have thou authority over ten cities.

And the ſecond came, ſaying, Lord, thy pound hath gained five pounds.

And he ſaid likewiſe to him, Be thou alſo over five cities.

And another came, faying, Lord, behold, here is thy pound, which I have kept laid up in a napkin:

For I feared thee, becaufe thou art an auftere man; thou takeft up that thou layedft not down, and reapeft that thou didft not fow.

And he faith unto him, Out of thine own mouth will I judge thee, thou wicked fervant. Thou kneweft that I was an auftere man, taking up that I laid not down, and reaping that I did not fow:

Wherefore then gaveft not thou my money into the bank, that at my coming I might have required mine own with ufury?

And he faid unto them that ftood by, Take from him the pound, and give it to him that hath ten pounds.

(And they faid unto him, Lord, he hath ten pounds.)

For I fay unto you, That unto every one which hath fhall be given; and from him that hath not, even that he hath fhall be taken away from him.

But thofe mine enemies, which would not that
I fhould reign over them, bring hither,
and flay them before me.

Luke, Chap. xix.
v. xii.—xxvii.

71

The Parable of the Good Shepherd.

VERILY, verily, I fay unto you, He that entereth not by the door into the fheepfold, but climbeth up fome other way, the fame is a thief and a robber.

But he that entereth in by the door is the fhepherd of the fheep.

To him the porter openeth; and the fheep hear his voice: and he calleth his own fheep by name, and leadeth them out.

And when he putteth forth his own fheep, he goeth before them, and the fheep follow him: for they know his voice.

And a ftranger will they not follow, but will flee from him: for they know not the voice of ftrangers.

This parable fpake Jefus unto them; but they underftood not what things they were which he fpake unto them.

Then faid Jefus unto them again, Verily, verily, I fay unto you, I am the door of the fheep.

All that ever came before me are thieves and robbers: but the fheep did not hear them.

I am the door: by me if any man enter in, he fhall be faved, and fhall go in and out, and find pafture.

The Good Shepherd.

The thief cometh not, but for to fteal, and to kill, and to deftroy: I am come that they might have life, and that they might have it more abundantly.

I am the good fhepherd: the good fhepherd giveth his life for the fheep.

But he that is an hireling, and not the fhepherd, whofe own the fheep are not, feeth the wolf coming, and leaveth the fheep, and fleeth: and the wolf catcheth them, and fcattereth the fheep.

The hireling fleeth, becaufe he is an hireling, and careth not for the fheep.

I am the good fhepherd, and know my fheep, and am known of mine.

As the Father knoweth me, even fo know I the Father: and I lay down my life for the fheep.

And other fheep I have, which are not of this fold: them alfo I must bring, and they fhall hear my voice; and there fhall be one fold, and one fhepherd.

Therefore doth my Father love me, becaufe I lay down my life, that I might take it again.

No man taketh it from me, but I lay it down of myfelf. I have power to lay it down, and I have power to take it again. This commandment have I received of my Father.

John, Chap. x.
v. i.—xviii.

The Parable of the True Vine.

I AM the true vine, and my Father is the huſband-man.

Every branch in me that beareth not fruit he taketh away: and every branch that beareth fruit, he purgeth it, that it may bring forth more fruit.

Now ye are clean through the word which I have ſpoken unto you.

Abide in me, and I in you. As the branch cannot bear fruit of itſelf, except it abide in the vine; no more can ye, except ye abide in me.

I am the vine, ye are the branches: He that abideth in me, and I in him, the ſame bringeth forth much fruit: for without me ye can do nothing.

If a man abide not in me, he is caſt forth as a branch, and is withered; and men gather them, and caſt them into the fire, and they are burned.

If ye abide in me, and my words abide in you, ye ſhall aſk what ye will, and it ſhall be done unto you.

Herein is my Father glorified, that ye bear much fruit; ſo ſhall ye be my diſciples.

As the Father hath loved me, ſo have I loved you: continue ye in my love.

If ye keep my commandments, ye fhall abide in my love; even as I have kept my Father's commandments, and abide in his love.

Thefe things have I fpoken unto you, that my joy might remain in you, and that your joy might be full.

This is my commandment, That ye love one another, as I have loved you.

Greater love hath no man than this, that a man lay down his life for his friends.

Ye are my friends, if ye do whatfoever I command you.

Henceforth I call you not fervants; for the fervant knoweth not what his lord doeth: but I have called you friends; for all things that I have heard of my Father I have made known unto you.

Ye have not chofen me, but I have chofen you, and ordained you, that ye fhould go and bring forth fruit, and
that your fruit fhould remain : that whatfoever
ye fhall afk of the Father in my name,
he may give it you.

John, Chap. xv.
v. i —xvi.

A CATALOGUE OF SELECTED DOVER BOOKS
IN ALL FIELDS OF INTEREST

A CATALOGUE OF SELECTED DOVER BOOKS
IN ALL FIELDS OF INTEREST

AMERICA'S OLD MASTERS, James T. Flexner. Four men emerged unexpectedly from provincial 18th century America to leadership in European art: Benjamin West, J. S. Copley, C. R. Peale, Gilbert Stuart. Brilliant coverage of lives and contributions. Revised, 1967 edition. 69 plates. 365pp. of text.

21806-6 Paperbound $3.00

FIRST FLOWERS OF OUR WILDERNESS: AMERICAN PAINTING, THE COLONIAL PERIOD, James T. Flexner. Painters, and regional painting traditions from earliest Colonial times up to the emergence of Copley, West and Peale Sr., Foster, Gustavus Hesselius, Feke, John Smibert and many anonymous painters in the primitive manner. Engaging presentation, with 162 illustrations. xxii + 368pp.

22180-6 Paperbound $3.50

THE LIGHT OF DISTANT SKIES: AMERICAN PAINTING, 1760-1835, James T. Flexner. The great generation of early American painters goes to Europe to learn and to teach: West, Copley, Gilbert Stuart and others. Allston, Trumbull, Morse; also contemporary American painters—primitives, derivatives, academics—who remained in America. 102 illustrations. xiii + 306pp.

22179-2 Paperbound $3.50

A HISTORY OF THE RISE AND PROGRESS OF THE ARTS OF DESIGN IN THE UNITED STATES, William Dunlap. Much the richest mine of information on early American painters, sculptors, architects, engravers, miniaturists, etc. The only source of information for scores of artists, the major primary source for many others. Unabridged reprint of rare original 1834 edition, with new introduction by James T. Flexner, and 394 new illustrations. Edited by Rita Weiss. 6⅝ x 9⅝.

21695-0, 21696-9, 21697-7 Three volumes, Paperbound $15.00

EPOCHS OF CHINESE AND JAPANESE ART, Ernest F. Fenollosa. From primitive Chinese art to the 20th century, thorough history, explanation of every important art period and form, including Japanese woodcuts; main stress on China and Japan, but Tibet, Korea also included. Still unexcelled for its detailed, rich coverage of cultural background, aesthetic elements, diffusion studies, particularly of the historical period. 2nd, 1913 edition. 242 illustrations. lii + 439pp. of text.

20364-6, 20365-4 Two volumes, Paperbound $6.00

THE GENTLE ART OF MAKING ENEMIES, James A. M. Whistler. Greatest wit of his day deflates Oscar Wilde, Ruskin, Swinburne; strikes back at inane critics, exhibitions, art journalism; aesthetics of impressionist revolution in most striking form. Highly readable classic by great painter. Reproduction of edition designed by Whistler. Introduction by Alfred Werner. xxxvi + 334pp.

21875-9 Paperbound $3.00

ALPHABETS AND ORNAMENTS, Ernst Lehner. Well-known pictorial source for decorative alphabets, script examples, cartouches, frames, decorative title pages, calligraphic initials, borders, similar material. 14th to 19th century, mostly European. Useful in almost any graphic arts designing, varied styles. 750 illustrations. 256pp. 7 x 10. 21905-4 Paperbound $4.00

PAINTING: A CREATIVE APPROACH, Norman Colquhoun. For the beginner simple guide provides an instructive approach to painting: major stumbling blocks for beginner; overcoming them, technical points; paints and pigments; oil painting; watercolor and other media and color. New section on "plastic" paints. Glossary. Formerly *Paint Your Own Pictures.* 221pp. 22000-1 Paperbound $1.75

THE ENJOYMENT AND USE OF COLOR, Walter Sargent. Explanation of the relations between colors themselves and between colors in nature and art, including hundreds of little-known facts about color values, intensities, effects of high and low illumination, complementary colors. Many practical hints for painters, references to great masters. 7 color plates, 29 illustrations. x + 274pp. 20944-X Paperbound $3.00

THE NOTEBOOKS OF LEONARDO DA VINCI, compiled and edited by Jean Paul Richter. 1566 extracts from original manuscripts reveal the full range of Leonardo's versatile genius: all his writings on painting, sculpture, architecture, anatomy, astronomy, geography, topography, physiology, mining, music, etc., in both Italian and English, with 186 plates of manuscript pages and more than 500 additional drawings. Includes studies for the Last Supper, the lost Sforza monument, and other works. Total of xlvii + 866pp. 7⅞ x 10¾. 22572-0, 22573-9 Two volumes, Paperbound $12.00

MONTGOMERY WARD CATALOGUE OF 1895. Tea gowns, yards of flannel and pillow-case lace, stereoscopes, books of gospel hymns, the New Improved Singer Sewing Machine, side saddles, milk skimmers, straight-edged razors, high-button shoes, spittoons, and on and on . . . listing some 25,000 items, practically all illustrated. Essential to the shoppers of the 1890's, it is our truest record of the spirit of the period. Unaltered reprint of Issue No. 57, Spring and Summer 1895. Introduction by Boris Emmet. Innumerable illustrations. xiii + 624pp. 8½ x 11⅝. 22377-9 Paperbound $8.50

THE CRYSTAL PALACE EXHIBITION ILLUSTRATED CATALOGUE (LONDON, 1851). One of the wonders of the modern world—the Crystal Palace Exhibition in which all the nations of the civilized world exhibited their achievements in the arts and sciences—presented in an equally important illustrated catalogue. More than 1700 items pictured with accompanying text—ceramics, textiles, cast-iron work, carpets, pianos, sleds, razors, wall-papers, billiard tables, beehives, silverware and hundreds of other artifacts—represent the focal point of Victorian culture in the Western World. Probably the largest collection of Victorian decorative art ever assembled—indispensable for antiquarians and designers. Unabridged republication of the Art-Journal Catalogue of the Great Exhibition of 1851, with all terminal essays. New introduction by John Gloag, F.S.A. xxxiv + 426pp. 9 x 12. 22503-8 Paperbound $5.00

A HISTORY OF COSTUME, Carl Köhler. Definitive history, based on surviving pieces of clothing primarily, and paintings, statues, etc. secondarily. Highly readable text, supplemented by 594 illustrations of costumes of the ancient Mediterranean peoples, Greece and Rome, the Teutonic prehistoric period; costumes of the Middle Ages, Renaissance, Baroque, 18th and 19th centuries. Clear, measured patterns are provided for many clothing articles. Approach is practical throughout. Enlarged by Emma von Sichart. 464pp.   21030-8 Paperbound $3.50

ORIENTAL RUGS, ANTIQUE AND MODERN, Walter A. Hawley. A complete and authoritative treatise on the Oriental rug—where they are made, by whom and how, designs and symbols, characteristics in detail of the six major groups, how to distinguish them and how to buy them. Detailed technical data is provided on periods, weaves, warps, wefts, textures, sides, ends and knots, although no technical background is required for an understanding. 11 color plates, 80 halftones, 4 maps. vi + 320pp. 6⅛ x 9⅛.   22366-3 Paperbound $5.00

TEN BOOKS ON ARCHITECTURE, Vitruvius. By any standards the most important book on architecture ever written. Early Roman discussion of aesthetics of building, construction methods, orders, sites, and every other aspect of architecture has inspired, instructed architecture for about 2,000 years. Stands behind Palladio, Michelangelo, Bramante, Wren, countless others. Definitive Morris H. Morgan translation. 68 illustrations. xii + 331pp.   20645-9 Paperbound . $3.00

THE FOUR BOOKS OF ARCHITECTURE, Andrea Palladio. Translated into every major Western European language in the two centuries following its publication in 1570, this has been one of the most influential books in the history of architecture. Complete reprint of the 1738 Isaac Ware edition. New introduction by Adolf Placzek, Columbia Univ. 216 plates. xxii + 110pp. of text. 9½ x 12¾.
                       21308-0 Clothbound $12.50

STICKS AND STONES: A STUDY OF AMERICAN ARCHITECTURE AND CIVILIZATION, Lewis Mumford.One of the great classics of American cultural history. American architecture from the medieval-inspired earliest forms to the early 20th century; evolution of structure and style, and reciprocal influences on environment. 21 photographic illustrations. 238pp.   20202-X Paperbound $2.00

THE AMERICAN BUILDER'S COMPANION, Asher Benjamin. The most widely used early 19th century architectural style and source book, for colonial up into Greek Revival periods. Extensive development of geometry of carpentering, construction of sashes, frames, doors, stairs; plans and elevations of domestic and other buildings. Hundreds of thousands of houses were built according to this book, now invaluable to historians, architects, restorers, etc. 1827 edition. 59 plates. 114pp. 7⅞ x 10¾.
                       22236-5 Paperbound $4.00

DUTCH HOUSES IN THE HUDSON VALLEY BEFORE 1776, Helen Wilkinson Reynolds. The standard survey of the Dutch colonial house and outbuildings, with constructional features, decoration, and local history associated with individual homesteads. Introduction by Franklin D. Roosevelt. Map. 150 illustrations. 469pp. 6⅝ x 9¼.   21469-9 Paperbound $5.00

JOHANN SEBASTIAN BACH, Philipp Spitta. One of the great classics of musicology, this definitive analysis of Bach's music (and life) has never been surpassed. Lucid, nontechnical analyses of hundreds of pieces (30 pages devoted to St. Matthew Passion, 26 to B Minor Mass). Also includes major analysis of 18th-century music. 450 musical examples. 40-page musical supplement. Total of xx + 1799pp.

(EUK) 22278-0, 22279-9 Two volumes, Clothbound $25.00

MOZART AND HIS PIANO CONCERTOS, Cuthbert Girdlestone. The only full-length study of an important area of Mozart's creativity. Provides detailed analyses of all 23 concertos, traces inspirational sources. 417 musical examples. Second edition. 509pp.

21271-8 Paperbound $4.50

THE PERFECT WAGNERITE: A COMMENTARY ON THE NIBLUNG'S RING, George Bernard Shaw. Brilliant and still relevant criticism in remarkable essays on Wagner's Ring cycle, Shaw's ideas on political and social ideology behind the plots, role of Leitmotifs, vocal requisites, etc. Prefaces. xxi + 136pp.

(USO) 21707-8 Paperbound $1.75

DON GIOVANNI, W. A. Mozart. Complete libretto, modern English translation; biographies of composer and librettist; accounts of early performances and critical reaction. Lavishly illustrated. All the material you need to understand and appreciate this great work. Dover Opera Guide and Libretto Series; translated and introduced by Ellen Bleiler. 92 illustrations. 209pp.

21134-7 Paperbound $2.00

BASIC ELECTRICITY, U. S. Bureau of Naval Personel. Originally a training course, best non-technical coverage of basic theory of electricity and its applications. Fundamental concepts, batteries, circuits, conductors and wiring techniques, AC and DC, inductance and capacitance, generators, motors, transformers, magnetic amplifiers, synchros, servomechanisms, etc. Also covers blue-prints, electrical diagrams, etc. Many questions, with answers. 349 illustrations. x + 448pp. 6½ x 9¼.

20973-3 Paperbound $3.50

REPRODUCTION OF SOUND, Edgar Villchur. Thorough coverage for laymen of high fidelity systems, reproducing systems in general, needles, amplifiers, preamps, loudspeakers, feedback, explaining physical background. "A rare talent for making technicalities vividly comprehensible," R. Darrell, *High Fidelity*. 69 figures. iv + 92pp.

21515-6 Paperbound $1.35

HEAR ME TALKIN' TO YA: THE STORY OF JAZZ AS TOLD BY THE MEN WHO MADE IT, Nat Shapiro and Nat Hentoff. Louis Armstrong, Fats Waller, Jo Jones, Clarence Williams, Billy Holiday, Duke Ellington, Jelly Roll Morton and dozens of other jazz greats tell how it was in Chicago's South Side, New Orleans, depression Harlem and the modern West Coast as jazz was born and grew. xvi + 429pp.

21726-4 Paperbound $3.95

FABLES OF AESOP, translated by Sir Roger L'Estrange. A reproduction of the very rare 1931 Paris edition; a selection of the most interesting fables, together with 50 imaginative drawings by Alexander Calder. v + 128pp. 6½x9¼.

21780-9 Paperbound $1.50

AGAINST THE GRAIN (A REBOURS), Joris K. Huysmans. Filled with weird images, evidences of a bizarre imagination, exotic experiments with hallucinatory drugs, rich tastes and smells and the diversions of its sybarite hero Duc Jean des Esseintes, this classic novel pushed 19th-century literary decadence to its limits. Full unabridged edition. Do not confuse this with abridged editions generally sold. Introduction by Havelock Ellis. xlix + 206pp.   22190-3 Paperbound $2.50

VARIORUM SHAKESPEARE: HAMLET. Edited by Horace H. Furness; a landmark of American scholarship. Exhaustive footnotes and appendices treat all doubtful words and phrases, as well as suggested critical emendations throughout the play's history. First volume contains editor's own text, collated with all Quartos and Folios. Second volume contains full first Quarto, translations of Shakespeare's sources (Belleforest, and Saxo Grammaticus), Der Bestrafte Brudermord, and many essays on critical and historical points of interest by major authorities of past and present. Includes details of staging and costuming over the years. By far the best edition available for serious students of Shakespeare. Total of xx + 905pp.
          21004-9, 21005-7, 2 volumes, Paperbound $7.00

A LIFE OF WILLIAM SHAKESPEARE, Sir Sidney Lee. This is the standard life of Shakespeare, summarizing everything known about Shakespeare and his plays. Incredibly rich in material, broad in coverage, clear and judicious, it has served thousands as the best introduction to Shakespeare. 1931 edition. 9 plates. xxix + 792pp.   21967-4 Paperbound $4.50

MASTERS OF THE DRAMA, John Gassner. Most comprehensive history of the drama in print, covering every tradition from Greeks to modern Europe and America, including India, Far East, etc. Covers more than 800 dramatists, 2000 plays, with biographical material, plot summaries, theatre history, criticism, etc. "Best of its kind in English," *New Republic*. 77 illustrations. xxii + 890pp.
          20100-7 Clothbound $10.00

THE EVOLUTION OF THE ENGLISH LANGUAGE, George McKnight. The growth of English, from the 14th century to the present. Unusual, non-technical account presents basic information in very interesting form: sound shifts, change in grammar and syntax, vocabulary growth, similar topics. Abundantly illustrated with quotations. Formerly *Modern English in the Making*. xii + 590pp.
          21932-1 Paperbound $3.50

AN ETYMOLOGICAL DICTIONARY OF MODERN ENGLISH, Ernest Weekley. Fullest, richest work of its sort, by foremost British lexicographer. Detailed word histories, including many colloquial and archaic words; extensive quotations. Do not confuse this with the Concise Etymological Dictionary, which is much abridged. Total of xxvii + 830pp. 6½ x 9¼.
          21873-2, 21874-0 Two volumes, Paperbound $7.90

FLATLAND: A ROMANCE OF MANY DIMENSIONS, E. A. Abbott. Classic of science-fiction explores ramifications of life in a two-dimensional world, and what happens when a three-dimensional being intrudes. Amusing reading, but also useful as introduction to thought about hyperspace. Introduction by Banesh Hoffmann. 16 illustrations. xx + 103pp.   20001-9 Paperbound $1.00

MATHEMATICAL PUZZLES FOR BEGINNERS AND ENTHUSIASTS, Geoffrey Mott-Smith. 189 puzzles from easy to difficult—involving arithmetic, logic, algebra, properties of digits, probability, etc.—for enjoyment and mental stimulus. Explanation of mathematical principles behind the puzzles. 135 illustrations. viii + 248pp.
20198-8 Paperbound $2.00

PAPER FOLDING FOR BEGINNERS, William D. Murray and Francis J. Rigney. Easiest book on the market, clearest instructions on making interesting, beautiful origami. Sail boats, cups, roosters, frogs that move legs, bonbon boxes, standing birds, etc. 40 projects; more than 275 diagrams and photographs. 94pp.
20713-7 Paperbound $1.00

TRICKS AND GAMES ON THE POOL TABLE, Fred Herrmann. 79 tricks and games—some solitaires, some for two or more players, some competitive games—to entertain you between formal games. Mystifying shots and throws, unusual caroms, tricks involving such props as cork, coins, a hat, etc. Formerly *Fun on the Pool Table*. 77 figures. 95pp.
21814-7 Paperbound $1.25

HAND SHADOWS TO BE THROWN UPON THE WALL: A SERIES OF NOVEL AND AMUSING FIGURES FORMED BY THE HAND, Henry Bursill. Delightful picturebook from great-grandfather's day shows how to make 18 different hand shadows: a bird that flies, duck that quacks, dog that wags his tail, camel, goose, deer, boy, turtle, etc. Only book of its sort. vi + 33pp. 6½ x 9¼. 21779-5 Paperbound $1.00

WHITTLING AND WOODCARVING, E. J. Tangerman. 18th printing of best book on market. "If you can cut a potato you can carve" toys and puzzles, chains, chessmen, caricatures, masks, frames, woodcut blocks, surface patterns, much more. Information on tools, woods, techniques. Also goes into serious wood sculpture from Middle Ages to present, East and West. 464 photos, figures. x + 293pp.
20965-2 Paperbound $2.50

HISTORY OF PHILOSOPHY, Julián Marias. Possibly the clearest, most easily followed, best planned, most useful one-volume history of philosophy on the market; neither skimpy nor overfull. Full details on system of every major philosopher and dozens of less important thinkers from pre-Socratics up to Existentialism and later. Strong on many European figures usually omitted. Has gone through dozens of editions in Europe. 1966 edition, translated by Stanley Appelbaum and Clarence Strowbridge. xviii + 505pp. 21739-6 Paperbound $3.50

YOGA: A SCIENTIFIC EVALUATION, Kovoor T. Behanan. Scientific but non-technical study of physiological results of yoga exercises; done under auspices of Yale U. Relations to Indian thought, to psychoanalysis, etc. 16 photos. xxiii + 270pp.
20505-3 Paperbound $2.50

Prices subject to change without notice.
Available at your book dealer or write for free catalogue to Dept. GI, Dover Publications, Inc., 180 Varick St., N. Y., N. Y. 10014. Dover publishes more than 150 books each year on science, elementary and advanced mathematics, biology, music, art, literary history, social sciences and other areas.